THIS JOURNAL BELONGS TO

www.ingramcontent.com/pod-product-compliance
Lightning Source LLC
Chambersburg PA
CBHW030718220526
45463CB00005B/2099
9781690130987